LOST AND FOUND

POMPEII
AND OTHER
Lost Cities

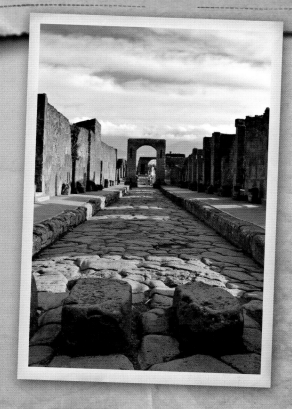

JOHN MALAM

QEB Publishing

Project Editor Carey Scott
Designer Stefan Morris Design
Illustrations The Art Agency
and MW Digital Graphics
Picture Researcher Maria Joannou

Front cover image: A mosaic floor, showing
Alexander the Great riding into battle, from a
villa in Pompeii.

Library of Congress Cataloging-in-Publication Data
Malam, John, 1957-
Pompeii and other lost cities / John Malam.
    p. cm. -- (Lost and found)
Includes index.
Summary: "Describes the historical circumstances that led to cities such as Pompeii and Machu
Picchu being lost and the archaeological discoveries that found evidence of these cities"
--Provided by publisher.
ISBN 978-1-60992-051-7 (library binding)
1. Extinct cities--Juvenile literature.
2. Civilization, Ancient--Juvenile literature.
3. Excavations (Archaeology)--Juvenile
literature. I. Title.
CC176.M35 2012
930.1--dc22

2011011266

Picture credits

Key: t=top, b=bottom, r=right, l=left, c=center
Alamy Images David Lyons 15t, Lou McGill 15b, David Lyons 30t; The Art Agency Ian Jackson 11b, 14b,
18b, 22b; Bridgeman Art Library British Museum, London, UK 12b, Collection of the New-York Historical
Society, USA 19t, World Religions Photo Library 23b, Ancient Art and Architecture Collection Ltd 25b, British
Museum, London, UK 32; Corbis Adam Woolfitt 3, Michael DeFreitas/Robert Harding World Imagery 4b,
Reuters Photographer/Reuters 5t, Roger Ressmeyer 9b, Sandro Vannini 11t, Gianni Dagli Orti 12t, 13l, Nathan
Benn/Ottochrome 16l, Adam Woolfitt 17t, John Garrett 17b, Yann Arthus-Bertrand 27b; Getty Images Gallo
Images/Danita Delimont 8b, Lloyd Kenneth Townsend, Jr./National Geographic 26b, De Agostini Picture
Library 28t, 29; Photolibrary Robert Harding Travel 2r, The British Library 4t, De Agostini Editore 10b, Robert
Harding Travel 25t, De Agostini Editore 27t; The Picture Desk Art Archive/Bibliothèque des Arts Décoratifs
Paris/Gianni Dagli Orti 6b, 7b; Shutterstock Peter Zaharov 1r, Bragin Alexey 2l, Peter Zaharov 8t, Vladimir
Wrangel 13r, Jule_Berlin 16, Steffen Foerster Photography 20t, Damian Gil 21, 31t, Vladimir Wrangel 31;
Topham Picturepoint 24, The Image Works 5b, Alinari 9t, The Granger Collection 19b, 20b, Luisa Ricciarini
23t, Duby Tal/Albatross 28b, The Granger Collection 30b. All maps by Mark Walker at MW Digital Graphics

The words in **bold** are explained in the Glossary on page 31.

CONTENTS

What is a Lost City? 4

LOST: A Roman Town 6
FOUND: Pompeii 8

LOST: Ancient Egyptian City 10
FOUND: Amarna 12

LOST: A Prehistoric Village 14
FOUND: Skara Brae 16

LOST: An Inca City 18
FOUND: Machu Picchu 20

LOST: Indus Valley Cities 22
FOUND: Mohenjo-daro 24

LOST: Minoan Town 26
FOUND: Akrotiri 28

Timeline of Discoveries 30
Glossary 31
Index 32

WHAT IS A LOST CITY?

It might seem hard to believe, but many cities and towns have vanished without a trace. When they are built near volcanoes, eruptions can bury them in ash. In deserts, strong winds might cover cities with sand, and flooded rivers can leave them buried under a thick layer of sediment. When disasters such as these occur, people abandon their cities for good.

There are lost cities all over the world. Some, such as Mohenjo-daro, Pakistan, and Pompeii, Italy, were lost thousands of years ago. Others, such as Machu Picchu, the famous Lost City of the Incas in Peru, were inhabited in more recent times, and then abandoned by their inhabitants and forgotten.

▼ In 1692, a powerful earthquake struck the island of Jamaica. The town of Port Royal was destroyed, and most of it was plunged to the bottom of the ocean.

▼ Machu Picchu is high up in the mountains of Peru. It was built by the Inca people in the 1400s, but they soon abandoned it—no one knows why. The Lost City of the Incas was discovered in 1911.

Frozen in time, lost cities are filled with clues about what really happened in history. For **archeologists**, they are a chance to go back in time and find out about the people who lived, worked, and died in them. Many lost cities have become tourist attractions and are visited by tens of thousands of people every year. Looking after them is a huge job, because it is important to keep them in good condition for future generations to enjoy.

▲ Large parts of the ancient city of Alexandria, Egypt, now lie beneath the Mediterranean Sea. Archeologists have recovered many Egyptian and Roman statues from the seabed.

Ghost Towns

Unlike lost cities, ghost towns, such as Bodie, California, have not been forgotten. People have always known about them, and where to find them. The thing ghost towns have in common with lost cities is that no one lives in them any more. Bodie was established as a gold mining town in 1859, and over the following 50 years lots of people moved there in the hope of becoming rich. But its last mine was closed in 1942 and Bodie became a ghost town.

LOST:
A ROMAN TOWN

The 20,000 Romans whose home was Pompeii were living in the shadow of a volcano. Looming over the town was a tall, cone-shaped hill—Mount Vesuvius. Vineyards usually thrived in the rich soil on the slopes of Vesuvius. But the year CE 79 was different.

Location: Pompeii, Italy
Date: August 24, CE 79

The grapes were dying on the vines. Wisps of steam and smoke came out of the ground, the air smelled of rotten eggs, and dead fish floated in the River Sarno. People were puzzled, and when a small earthquake rocked the town on August 20, they became frightened. Then, four days later, they watched in horror as a dirty gray cloud rose from the summit of the oddly shaped hill. Only then did they realize that Vesuvius was a volcano, waking up after a long, long sleep.

All that day, ash fell from the cloud, covering Pompeii's streets. Most people fled to safety, but about 2,000 stayed behind. By late afternoon, hard pieces of pumice were raining down, and roofs were collapsing under the weight. Late that night, tremors shook the ground, the booming of the volcano grew louder, and lightning flashed through the sky.

▼ A couple collecting water from a street fountain and a customer buying a snack at a "takeout" shop. Soon, everyday life in Pompeii would be ended forever.

Other Lost Towns

Pompeii was not the only town destroyed when Vesuvius erupted. The towns of Stabiae and Oplontis were also buried by ash, and Herculaneum was lost beneath a deep layer of mud. In the countryside around the volcano, countless farms and villas were wiped out. A vast area had become a disaster zone. People slowly returned and dug into the ruins, searching for their possessions. The Roman emperor Titus visited the area and ordered repairs to some towns, but nothing could be done for Pompeii.

Miles
Km 10

Herculaneum Mt. Vesuvius
Pompeii
Oplontis
Stabiae

Early the next morning, August 25, the ash cloud fell back to earth, creating waves of volcanic debris that flowed down the sides of Vesuvius. Pompeii was 5 miles (8 kilometers) away, but the torrents of red-hot ash, **pumice**, and rock reached the town in minutes and smothered it. Pompeii was buried, and had become a lost city.

▼ When Vesuvius erupted, day turned to night. There was enough time for most people to escape, but those who stayed in their homes perished.

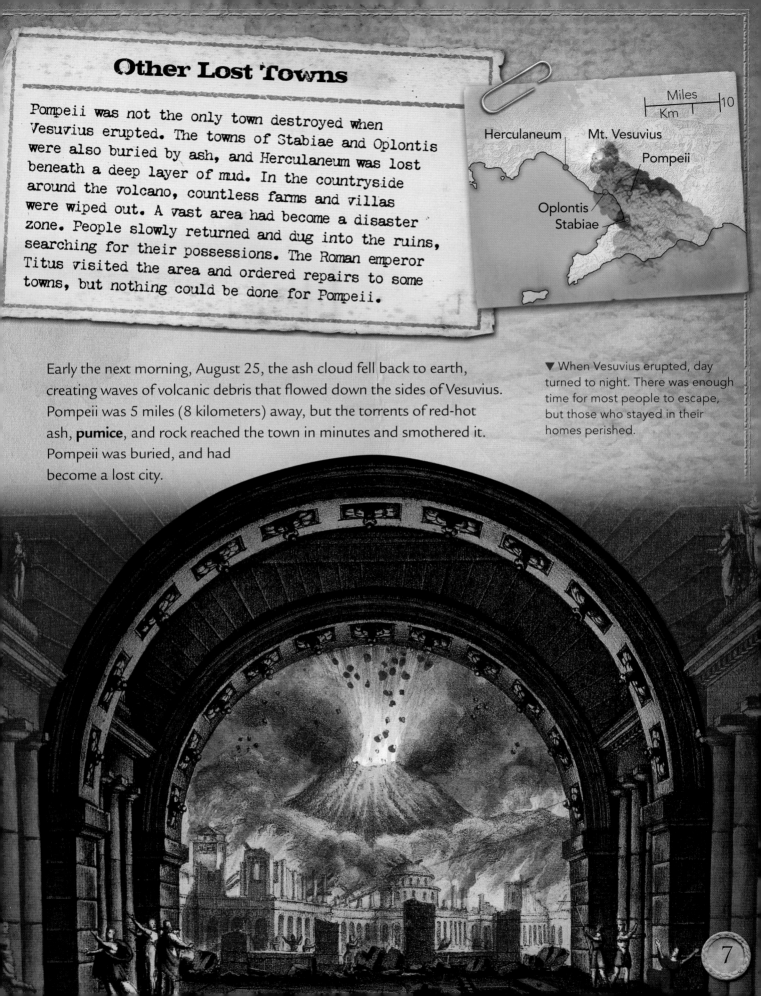

FOUND: POMPEII

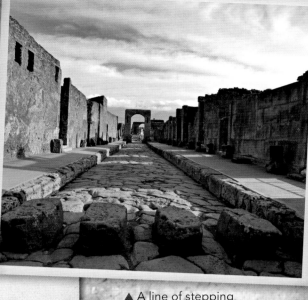

As the centuries passed, Pompeii became little more than a fuzzy memory. Eventually its name was forgotten, and local people called it just *la città*, meaning "the city." They knew something was buried deep under the ground, but they weren't sure what.

In the 1700s, it became fashionable for rich people in Europe to decorate their grand houses with ancient Greek and Roman statues. Collectors also wanted to get their hands on them. **Treasure hunters** realized they could make money by finding bronze and marble statues and selling them, and in the 1740s they started digging into *la città* in search of valuables. In 1763, one such treasure hunter unearthed a stone with Latin writing on it that solved the mystery of the city's real name. The stone said the city was called Pompeii.

▲ A line of stepping stones crosses a Pompeii street. Stray dogs roamed the streets, which were littered with rotting vegetables, animal dung, and other garbage.

Plaster People

When excavator Giuseppe Fiorelli was uncovering Pompeii in the 1860s, he came across strange holes in the ash layer. Curious, he pumped **plaster of Paris** into them until they were filled. Then, when the plaster had set hard, he removed the ash and got a surprise. The plaster had set into the shape of the bodies of people who had died in the disaster. Their real bodies and skeletons had disintegrated long before, but their ghostly outlines remained.

Excavators have cleared much of the ash that covered the city, and the Roman streets and buildings have come back to life. The excavators have found houses of the rich and poor, temples to the Roman gods, stores and bakeries, theaters, and the arena where gladiators fought. Pompeii is a complete Roman city that a **natural disaster** has preserved perfectly. It is as if time itself has stood still, with Pompeii untouched since the day it was lost, almost 2,000 years ago.

◄ This mosaic is from a house in Pompeii. It was intended to warn visitors to beware of the guard dog.

▼ Mount Vesuvius looms over the ruins of Pompeii. About 1,500 buildings are being preserved by archeologists.

LOST:
ANCIENT EGYPTIAN CITY

Akhenaten was a pharaoh (king) of ancient Egypt. He was not at all like the pharaohs who had ruled before him. He wanted to do things his way, not theirs, and because he was the pharaoh he could do anything he wanted.

Location: Amarna, Egypt
Date: about 1350 BCE

Within a few years of becoming **pharaoh**, Akhenaten gave the order to abandon the old capital of Thebes, and to close down its temples. A new capital city, called Akhetaten, was built 250 miles (400 kilometers) away, in the desert, close to the River Nile. Akhetaten was a huge city, measuring around four miles (seven kilometers) from end to end, and as many as 50,000 people may have lived there. Akhenaten had a magnificent palace built for himself and his family to live in. He had several children, one of whom may have been Tutankhamun. The city's rich people lived in fine houses with pools and gardens. There were lots of temples for people to worship in, and a district where the **craftspeople** lived and worked.

◄ Akhenaten became pharaoh of Egypt in about 1353 BCE and died after reigning for 17 years.

Aten the Sun God

At the start of his reign, the pharaoh was called Amenhotep, but he changed his name to Akhenaten after he made a big change to the religion of Egypt. No longer would there be many gods, he said, but only one god—the sun god Aten. He took the god's name for his own name, and became Akhenaten, meaning "servant of the Aten." He is shown here worshipping Aten with his family.

▼ The main palace at Akhetaten had hundreds of columns. Some, like these, were shaped like bundles of papyrus water reeds .

But the new capital was one of many changes ordered by Akhenaten, and most people did not like these changes. Soon after the pharaoh died, things went back to the way they had been before. Thebes became the capital city once again and its old temples were reopened. People left the new city of Akhetaten. They pulled down its buildings, and carried off the stone to be reused in other buildings. In time, what was left of the city was lost from sight as the desert sand blew in and covered the ruins.

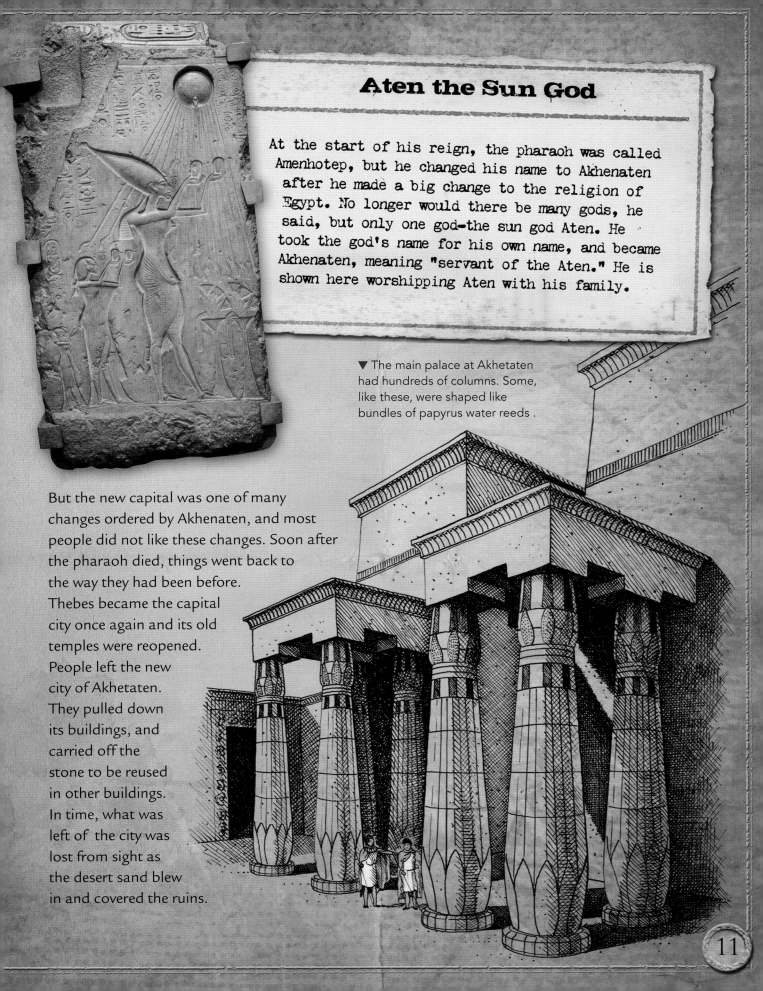

FOUND:

AMARNA

FACT FILE

The city of Akhetaten was lived in for only about 25 years before it was abandoned.

Today, the city of Akhetaten, abandoned 3,300 years ago, is known by the modern name of Amarna. Although it fell into ruins and many of its building stones were taken away, it is the best preserved Ancient Egyptian city.

In the 1790s, French soldiers made a plan of the city, which gave a rough idea of its size. The drawing was published in a book that described the **sites** and **monuments** of Ancient Egypt. From then on, people began to take an interest in Amarna. Artists visited the site and made sketches of its tombs, and experts made more detailed plans. Then, in 1887, a villager digging for *sebakh* —a rich earth used for farming and fuel—unearthed 300 ancient letters written on clay tablets. They were official documents sent from foreign lands that Ancient Egypt had links with, left behind when Amarna was abandoned.

▲ This is the tomb of Meryre, High Priest of the Aten, at Amarna. After the death of Akhenaten, the tomb was damaged by people who wanted to destroy images of the unpopular pharaoh and his officials.

◄ This colored glass container was found inside a house at Amarna. It represents a tilapia, a species of fish that lives in the River Nile.

News about the letters spread, and treasure hunters began to dig at Amarna, hoping to find other valuable items. Archeologists worried that the site would be **looted** so, in 1892, they began the long, slow job of uncovering the buried city. As the sand was cleared away, the remains of Akhenaten's palace, the temple to the sun god Aten, and houses of nobles and commoners were revealed. The work is far from over, and excavations are continuing today.

Amarna Letter

This is one of the many clay tablets found at Amarna in the 1330s. The wedge-shaped marks are called **cuneiform**. This writing was used by people who lived in lands northeast of Egypt. Experts have been able to decipher cuneiform, and the tablets are a valuable source of information about relations between pharaoh Akhenaten and rulers of nearby lands.

► This head of Nefertiti, Akhenaten's wife, was found in the storeroom of the royal sculptor Thutmose at Amarna. It is one of the greatest treasures of Ancient Egypt.

13

LOST:
A PREHISTORIC VILLAGE

Thousands of years ago, a little village disappeared. It was on the largest of the Orkney Islands, off the north coast of Scotland. Between 10 and 20 farming families lived there but, when something happened, they all abandoned their homes, leaving the village deserted.

Skara Brae, Orkney Islands
Date: about 2500 BCE

The village lay behind sand dunes, set back from the crashing waves of the Atlantic Ocean. Its stone, timber, and turf houses were huddled close together, with narrow, winding passageways running between them. The stone house walls were very thick. Inside, flat stones paved the floors, and even the beds and cupboards were made from stone. Fires burned in open hearths, and smoke drifted up and found its way out through the roof.

The villagers kept cattle, sheep, and pigs, and grew crops of wheat and barley. They ate shellfish and fish from the sea, and made oil for their lamps from the fat of whales and seals. Sometimes they ate seabirds and their eggs. Life had been this way for generations.

▼ A Skara Brae family prepare a meal of seabirds and shellfish. Experts are not sure what they would have used for fuel, but it is likely to have been dried seaweed.

No one knows exactly why the village was abandoned. The sand dunes between the village and the sea may have shifted, leaving the houses exposed to the wild waves rolling in from the Atlantic. Or a great storm may have swept the dunes over the village. All we know for sure is that the villagers left their homes. Sand blew in and filled the passageways, and the roofs of the houses collapsed. The drifting sand completely buried the houses, and all traces of the village were lost.

▲ The narrow passageways of Skara Brae can still be seen in the remains of the village. Some were roofed over, so that people had to bend over to walk along them.

Stone Furniture

Very few trees grow on the Orkney Islands, so the main building material has always been stone. It splits into flat slabs, which are perfect for stacking to make walls and pieces of furniture. The village houses had stone cupboards or dressers, like this one. Beds were made from slabs laid on their edges, probably filled with dried heather for sleeping on.

FOUND:
SKARA BRAE

No one knows whether
a storm buried the
prehistoric village,
but it was a storm
that uncovered
its remains. In the winter of 1850,
a severe gale roared in from the Atlantic
Ocean and stripped the grass off a high
sand dune known as Skara Brae.

▲ There are many prehistoric monuments in the Orkney Islands. The Ring of Brodgar is a large circle of standing stones, made at about the same time as Skara Brae.

When the storm died down, tons of sand had been blown away, and stone walls stood in its place. The storm also exposed a huge midden, or mound of garbage, made up of thousands of limpet shells. Orkney was well known for its **prehistoric** tombs and standing stones, but no one had seen anything like this before. Not surprisingly, the landowner was curious about what was buried on his land. He cleared away more of the dune, and as more stone walls and passages came into view, he realized he was looking at the remains of long-lost houses—but he couldn't tell how old they were.

In December 1924, the site was damaged when a winter storm washed away one of the ancient houses. Archeologists knew they had to act fast, or the next big storm could destroy everything. Over the next few years, they uncovered all the houses. They found pieces of pottery, beads from necklaces, animal bones, and stone tools used for cutting and scraping. These objects helped them put an age to the village, which they said was around 4,500 years.

▲ Craftspeople used the bones of seals and whales to make useful objects, such as these two spoons and a fork.

Strange Stones

Among the many objects found at Skara Brae were four stone balls carved into unusual shapes. Similar stones have been found at other prehistoric sites in Britain. They have been carefully and skillfully designed and carved. Experts can only guess why they were made, and what they were used for. They may have been religious or magical objects, or just pieces of decorative art.

▶ The roof of this house at Skara Brae disappeared long ago, but its layout is preserved. On the ground in the center of the house is a hearth where a fire would have burned.

FACT FILE

Skara Brae is the best preserved Neolithic village in northern Europe. The Neolithic Age lasted from about 4500 to 1700 BCE.

LOST:
AN INCA CITY

In the 1400s, the Inca people controlled a huge empire in South America. Their homeland was in present-day Peru, and their capital city was called Cuzco. To the northwest of Cuzco was a valley, and in its surrounding mountains the Incas built a fabulous estate for their emperor.

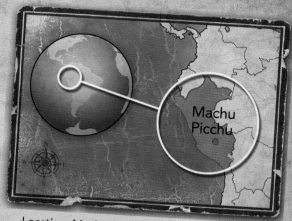

Location: Machu Picchu, Peru
Date: 1450s

Their emperor was called Pachacuti. He was a powerful leader, and under him the Incas conquered new lands until their empire stretched 2,500 miles (4,000 kilometers), from Colombia in the north to Chile in the south. In about 1450, they decided to build a royal estate for Pachacuti—a place where he could relax well away from the busy city of Cuzco. They chose to build the **estate** above the valley of the Urubamba River, a five-day walk from Cuzco.

▼ The Temple of the Sun was used to honor and celebrate Inti, the Inca sun god. Twice a year the sun shone through a window directly onto a large stone inside the temple.

Emperor Pachacuti

Pachacuti became emperor of the Incas in 1438. His name meant "Earth Shaker," and he ruled as a **warrior emperor** for 33 years. At the start of his long reign the Incas were a minor group of people in South America. But Pachacuti defeated neighboring groups, and by taking control of their land, he created the Inca empire. By the time of his death, Pachacuti had made the Incas the leading people in South America.

The Incas built more than 140 stone buildings on a high ridge between two sacred mountains, one of which was called Machu Picchu. In time, the royal estate itself was given the name Machu Picchu. Most of the time, only a few people lived at Machu Picchu, but when Pachacuti came to stay, about 1,000 people came too.

Pachacuti died in 1471. The Inca emperors who came after him used Machu Picchu too, but not for long. In 1532, Spanish invaders who had come to Peru in search of gold and other riches conquered the Inca empire. The Spanish looted many cities and towns, but not Machu Picchu —because they never found it. But, only around 100 years after they had built it, the defeated Incas abandoned Machu Picchu. The jungle closed in, and the buildings of Machu Picchu disappeared from sight.

◄ Spanish troops capture the last Inca emperor, Atahualpa. They executed him soon after, in 1533, bringing the mighty Inca empire to an end.

FOUND:
MACHU PICCHU

As the centuries passed, Machu Picchu stayed a secret, hidden place, known to only a few people. But as archeologists and explorers became interested in the Incas, they began searching for the ruins of their cities and towns in the forests and mountains of Peru.

In 1911, an American man named Hiram Bingham went to Peru to look for Inca ruins. He thought there might be some in an unexplored part of the valley of the Urubamba River. Bingham ventured into the dense jungle with a team of fellow explorers and porters who carried their equipment and bags. After several days of trekking, a farmer told Bingham about Inca ruins high up on a steep, jungle-clad mountain. With the farmer and a Peruvian soldier, Bingham set off to search for the ruins.

▲ Most of the buildings of Machu Picchu were constructed from stone blocks carefully cut to fit together without any binding material.

Hiram Bingham

Hiram Bingham (1875-1956) was a history teacher at Yale University in New Haven, Connecticut. He was interested in the history of South America, and was excited at the thought of finding lost Inca cities in unexplored parts of Peru. When he came to Machu Picchu, he thought he had found Vilcabamba, the last stronghold of the Incas. In fact, the lost city of Vilcabamba was in another valley.

They climbed for more than an hour, until they were among the clouds. A local boy joined them, and he led Bingham on the last part of the climb. To Bingham's amazement, they came to a series of terraces faced with stone, which seemed to rise up the mountain like giant steps. Then, as he pushed his way through bamboo thickets and tangled vines, Bingham came across walls, ruined houses, temples, and courtyards. Bingham later said he was "spellbound" at the sight. He went back several times over the next few years. As he cleared away the undergrowth and the poisonous snakes, the buildings of Machu Picchu were revealed. Bingham called it "The Lost City of the Incas."

▼ Machu Picchu's isolated mountain location is clear to see in this photograph. The Lost City of the Incas is almost 8,000 feet (2,400 meters) above sea level—high enough to cause altitude sickness in some people.

LOST:

INDUS VALLEY CITIES

Four thousand years ago, there were many busy cities along the banks of the Indus river, in present-day Pakistan. They were among the first true cities in the world but, one by one, they all vanished.

Location: Mohenjo-daro, Pakistan.
Date: about 2000 BCE

The cities were spread out over large areas, and thousands of people lived in them. Buildings were made from baked **mud brick** set out on a grid of streets. The cities were divided into districts with different purposes. Some areas were packed with workshops for craftspeople. Elsewhere were residential districts, and some of the houses there were sophisticated enough to have bathrooms, drainage systems, and their own private water supplies. In other parts of the cities were big public buildings, such as storehouses for wheat and barley. There were also buildings with large, open-air pools for bathing.

▼ Craftspeople at Mohenjo-daro worked with shell and bone. They made scoops or ladles from seashells, and sharpened animal bones to make needles for sewing.

▲ This baked clay model was found at Mohenjo-daro. It is a cart pulled by two oxen, and it may have been the precious toy of a child that lived in the city.

The Indus cities were busy and prosperous, and the biggest of all was home to 30,000 people. No one knows its real name, but today it is called Mohenjo-daro. Together with all the other cities, something happened that made Mohenjo-daro go into decline. Some experts think the climate changed and the cities were flooded. They do know that Mohenjo-daro became a city in a marshy lake. It was no longer a good place to live, and people drifted away, never to return.

The Great Bath

Bathing seems to have been important to the people of Mohenjo-daro. The city had an enormous bathhouse, with a deep pool that was almost 40 feet (12 meters) long and 23 feet (7 meters) wide. To keep the water from leaking away, the sides of the pool were coated in a type of tar called bitumen. Perhaps people believed the water here was holy, and by bathing in it they purified and cleansed their souls.

FOUND: MOHENJO-DARO

The ancient cities along the banks of the Indus were built from fragile mud brick. When the bricks crumbled and the buildings collapsed, mounds of earth were the only things left.

The earth mounds had their uses. In the 1850s, a railroad line was being built close to the village of Harappa. The builders needed a lot of packing material to put under the track, so they took thousands of old mud bricks from a nearby mound. They had no idea what the mound was, and neither did anyone else.

No one took much interest in the mound at Harappa, or in the others, until the 1920s. Only then did archeologists decide to take a proper look. **Excavations** began at Harappa, and at a larger mound 400 miles (645 kilometers) to the southwest. Local people called this mound Mohenjo-daro, meaning "Mound of the Dead." As the site was excavated, hundreds of buildings and streets were uncovered, and a lost city came into view. This came as a great surprise, as no one expected that a city this big had existed 4,000 years ago in this part of the world. The same happened at Harappa, and archeologists realized they had found not just another lost city, but an entire lost **civilization**. They called it the Indus civilization, after the great river on whose floodplain the cities had been built.

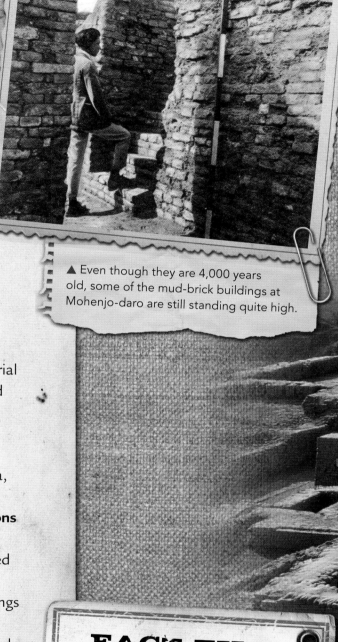

▲ Even though they are 4,000 years old, some of the mud-brick buildings at Mohenjo-daro are still standing quite high.

FACT FILE

Mohenjo-daro covers about 600 acres (243 hectares), around the size of 550 football fields—and less than 10 per cent of the city has been excavated.

Mystery Script

Thousands of small square carved stones have been found in the cities of the Indus civilization. The stones are carved with pictures below and signs above. There are about 400 different signs, which might stand for words or for sounds in words. Many experts have tried to interpret the signs but they have all failed. The Indus Valley script, as it is known, has remained an unsolved mystery.

▲ The buildings of Mohenjo-daro are very fragile, as wind and rain quickly wear away the ancient mud brick when it is exposed to the air. For this reason, archeologists have decided to leave most of the city buried.

LOST:
MINOAN TOWN

From the air, the islands of the Aegean Sea look like stones scattered across the clear blue water. But one fateful day 3,600 years ago, one of these peaceful islands was ripped apart, and a town was destroyed.

Location: Santorini, Greece.
Date: 1600 BCE

Thera was home to the people of the Minoan civilization. On the south side of the island was a small town which is today called Akrotiri. It had narrow streets and houses two and three stories high. They were made from stone and timber, and their walls were coated with smooth plaster on which brightly colored pictures were painted. Wheat and barley grew in nearby fields, and there were olive groves and vineyards. The townspeople kept sheep, goats, and cattle, and they caught fish and wild animals. They had a good life, but everything changed the day the ground shook.

▶ This aerial photograph of Thera, today called Santorini, shows the results of the volcanic eruption more than 3,500 years ago. The island looks as if a giant bite has been taken out of it.

◀ The ancient buildings of Akrotiri still stand almost to their full height, and this helps experts imagine how the town looked 3,600 years ago.

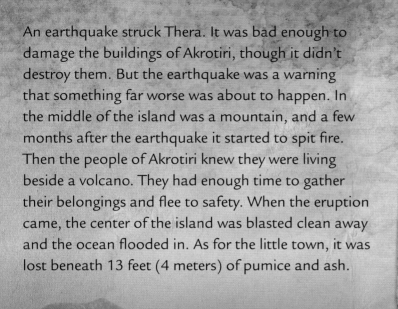

An earthquake struck Thera. It was bad enough to damage the buildings of Akrotiri, though it didn't destroy them. But the earthquake was a warning that something far worse was about to happen. In the middle of the island was a mountain, and a few months after the earthquake it started to spit fire. Then the people of Akrotiri knew they were living beside a volcano. They had enough time to gather their belongings and flee to safety. When the eruption came, the center of the island was blasted clean away and the ocean flooded in. As for the little town, it was lost beneath 13 feet (4 meters) of pumice and ash.

Is Thera Atlantis?

Plato was a famous philosopher, mathematician, and writer from ancient Greece. He wrote about a lost island called Atlantis, which was destroyed by earthquakes and sank without a trace. Ever since Plato wrote about it, people have wanted to find Atlantis. Some experts believe Thera is the place where Plato's idea of a lost island comes from, but others disagree.

FOUND:

AKROTIRI

The first signs of a buried town on Thera were found in the 1860s. In Egypt, work had begun on the Suez Canal—a massive building project that created a waterway between the Mediterranean Sea and the Red Sea. Vast quantities of cement were used to build the canal, and one of the raw materials needed to make cement was ash.

The canal builders got their ash from the island of Thera, where it lay in deep layers. As they removed the ash, the laborers came across a layer of stone blocks. It was clear they were pieces of cut and shaped stone, and must have been part of a building. Then, in 1870, an excavation was carried out close to the modern village of Akrotiri, and buried under the ash were the unmistakable signs of old buildings. Walls were decorated with paintings, and many pieces of pottery and animal bone were found. It looked as if a town might be buried under the ash, and people started talking about a "new Pompeii," after the Roman town in Italy (see page 6).

▲ Excavations have revealed box-shaped, flat-roofed houses that made up the residential part of Thera's lost town.

▶ The walls of many of the houses at Akrotiri were decorated with colorful frescoes, or wall paintings. This one shows two young boxers.

Volcanic Fallout

When the volcano on Thera erupted, it caused one of the biggest volcanic explosions in history. It is known that volcanic ash blew around 60 miles (100 kilometers) to the southeast of Thera, where it fell onto the Minoan towns and palaces on the island of Crete. The Minoan civilization came to a sudden end soon after. Could the Thera eruption have been the cause? Some experts believe so.

In 1967, almost 100 years after it was first found, archeologists began the job of uncovering the mystery town. They named it Akrotiri, after the nearby village. As they cleared the ash away, long-lost buildings came into view. To everyone's amazement, they were still standing almost to their full height. No skeletons were found, and very few valuable items turned up. This made archeologists think the inhabitants escaped, taking their valuables with them, before the volcano blew up.

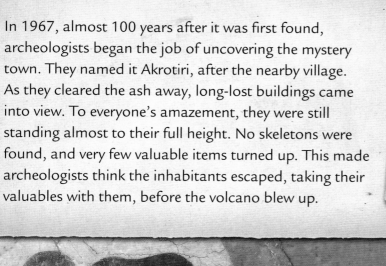

FACT FILE

Just one gold object was found at Akrotiri: a small figure of an animal called an ibex, which was hidden underneath a floor.

TIMELINE
OF DISCOVERIES

1763
An inscribed stone is found in the ruins of an ancient Roman town in the south of Italy, naming the town as Pompeii.

1790s
French soldiers in Egypt visit the site of Akhetaten, and draw up the first map showing the city's size and layout.

1850
A storm lashes the coast of the Orkney Islands, north of Scotland. It strips away part of a sand dune known as Skara Brae, revealing prehistoric stone houses.

1850s
The first remains of the lost cities of the Indus civilization are found in Pakistan.

1860s
Excavations at Pompeii reveal a large part of the buried Roman town.

1870
An excavation on the Greek island of Santorini uncovers part of an ancient town.

1911
Hiram Bingham finds Machu Picchu, the Lost City of the Incas.

1920s
Excavations begin at two ancient mounds in Pakistan. One mound is at Harappa, the other at Mohenjo-daro. They are the lost cities of the Indus civilization.

1924
Excavations begin at Skara Brae, Orkney, to uncover one of the earliest villages in Europe.

1967
Excavations begin on the Greek island of Santorini, and an ancient town is found. Archeologists name it Akrotiri.

1967
Archeologists find Pavlopetri, an ancient Greek city.

1994
Parts of the lost city of Alexandria, Egypt, are found submerged in the Mediterranean Sea.

2008
American and Peruvian explorers claim to have found the ruins of the lost Inca city of Paititi in Peru.

GLOSSARY

archeologist
A person who digs up and studies the remains of the past.

BCE
Used in dates. Means "Before the Common Era," which begins with year 1.

CE
Used in dates. Means "Common Era." The Common Era begins with year 1, which is the same as the year AD 1 in the Christian calendar.

civilization
To be called a civilization, a culture or society has to show signs of being advanced, such as having leaders, kings, writing, armies, or an organized religion.

craftspeople
People who are skilled at crafts, such as making pottery, jewelry, or textiles.

cuneiform (*q-nay-e-form*)
An ancient script (writing) used in Iraq, Iran, and neighboring countries.

estate
A large area of land owned by an important person, which is set aside for their personal use.

excavation
Careful digging into the ground to uncover remains of the past.

looted
Describes objects that are stolen in order to be sold.

monument
An old building, statue, or place that has been preserved because it is interesting or important.

mud brick
A building brick made from clay, often mixed with chopped grass, and dried by the sun.

natural disaster
A disaster caused by nature, such as an earthquake or volcanic eruption.

pharaoh
A king or queen of Ancient Egypt.

plaster of Paris
A sticky white paste that hardens when it sets (dries out). Used for pouring into spaces to make casts.

prehistoric
Before people developed writing and before written records were made.

pumice
A volcanic rock filled with air bubbles, making it very light.

site
An area where a building or a whole town once stood.

treasure hunter
A person who searches for treasure. Some treasure hunters damage ancient sites; others work with archeologists.

warrior emperor
A ruler who was also a fighter who led his people in war.

INDEX

Akhenaten 10, 11, 12, 13
Akhetaten 10, 11, 12–13, 30
Akrotiri 26–29, 30
Alexandria 5, 30
altitude sickness 21
Amarna (Akhetaten) 10, 11, 12–13, 30
archeologists 5, 9, 13, 16, 20, 29, 31
Atahualpa 19
Aten 11, 13
Atlantis 27

bathhouses 22, 23
Bingham, Hiram 20, 21
Bodie 5

clay models 23
clay tablets 12, 13
craftspeople 10, 16, 22, 31
cuneiform writing 13, 31
Cuzco 18

earthquakes 4, 6, 27
Egypt, Ancient 10–13
excavations 8, 9, 13, 24, 28, 31

floods 4, 23
frescoes (wall paintings) 26, 29

ghost towns 5
gold mining towns 5

Harappa 24, 30
Herculaneum 7

Incas 4, 18–21, 30
Indus civilization 24, 25, 30
Indus Valley 22–25
Indus Valley script 25

looters 13, 19, 31
lost cities 4–5

Machu Picchu 4, 18–21, 30
middens 16
Minoan civilization 26–29
Mohenjo-daro 4, 22, 23–25, 30
mosaics 9
Mount Vesuvius 6–7, 9
mud bricks 22, 24, 25, 31

Nefertiti 13
Neolithic Age 17

Oplontis 7
Orkney Islands 14–17

Pachacuti 18, 19
Paititi 30
Pavlopetri 30
pharaohs 10, 11, 12, 31
plaster casts 8
Plato 27
Pompeii 4, 6–9, 30

Port Royal 4
prehistoric village 14–17
pumice 6, 7, 27, 31

Ring of Brodgar 16
Romans 6–9

Skara Brae 14–17, 30
smallpox 21
Stabiae 7
standing stones 16
stone carvings 17, 25
Suez Canal 28

temples 9, 10, 13, 18
Thebes 10, 11
Thera (Santorini) 26–29, 30
tombs 12, 16
tourist attractions 5
treasure hunters 8, 13, 31
Tutankhamun 10

Vilcabamba 20
volcanic eruptions 4, 6–7, 26, 27, 28